Build Wealth, Eliminate Financial Mediocrity,

and Become Financially Independent

20 Strategies to Elevate

Your Financial

Outcomes

I0446828

Destiny S. Harris

. . .

Thank you for taking the time to read this book. As a token of my appreciation, here is a gift to you.

I give away free books daily. Here's how to get your free books today:

Step 1: Visit amazon.com/author/destinyharris

Step 2: Filter books by "Price: Low to High"

Step 3: Download available free books

. . .

Table of Contents

Disclaimer   12

A Thought   14

20 Strategies   16

Strategy 1   17

Strategy 2   20

Strategy 3   23

Strategy 4   25

Strategy 5   28

Strategy 6   31

Strategy 7   34

Strategy 8   37

Strategy 9   41

Strategy 10   43

Strategy 11   45

Strategy 12   47

Strategy 13   50

Strategy 14   52

Strategy 15   54

Strategy 16   56

Strategy 17   58

Strategy 18   61

Strategy 19   64

Strategy 20   67

Thank You For Reading   69

The End.   71

About Destiny S. Harris   74

Connect W/ Destiny S. Harris   78

Free Gifts!   80

. . .

. . .

Disclaimer

This book is for informational purposes only. It should not be considered Financial or Legal Advice. Not all information will be accurate. Consult a financial professional before making any significant financial decisions.

. . .

A Thought

Do you want to level up financially?

Implement the following 20 strategies and notice a change in your finances instantly. Some things just work; it's that simple.

. . .

20 Strategies

Strategy 1

1. Invest 15–25% or more of your income

That's right. Not 10% of your income. 15–25%+ of your income. I always believe 25% is a better way to go, but that's a personal preference. Your savings rate will grow as you acquire more income, and this will help you establish five things:

- Financial security
- Financial freedom
- Financial peace
- Financial discipline
- Financial elevation.

Most people save nothing **or** save around 10% of their income. Those who save around 10% of their income often still end up broke when retirement comes around. How does that work?

Because 10% of an average income will help you end up with average savings. Take the more aggressive approach when it comes to saving, and you'll end up a little bit happier in the end.

. . .

Strategy 2

2. Maintain a 2-year emergency fund

There is a minimum of 12 reasons to have a stocked and stacked 2-year emergency fund:

1: Peace of mind

2: Financial freedom

3: Mitigate job dependency

4: Be prepared for most emergencies

5: Have liquid assets that are easily accessible

6: Cover any living expenses for two years

7: Recession-proof your finances

8: Focus on investing

9: Never be broke

10: A 3–6-month emergency fund goes by quickly

11: Have enough resources to more than scrape by

12: Take time off

. . .

Strategy 3

3. Live below your means

This **is** the most salient financial strategy to implement. If you implement this one strategy, you guarantee yourself almost 99% success financially.

When you live below your means, you will always have money in the bank. You will remain out of debt and avoid living paycheck to paycheck.

. . .

Strategy 4

4. Live debt-free

Here are the most common types of debt [see immediately below]. You probably have at least one or more of these types of debts, or you've probably *had* one or more of these types of debts at some point. The majority **maintains** debt instead of eradicating debt.

- Credit card debt

- Student loans

- Car loans

- Personal loans

- Medical bills

- Property loans

You can do the opposite of the majority and live **without** debt; it's an unusual way to live but also an exhilarating and liberating manner of living. Owe no one anything.

Proverbs 6:1–7 says, "If you've signed surety, my son, do this. Give no sleep to your eyelids, no slumber to your eyes, and deliver yourself like a gazelle from the hand of the hunter [..]." A powerful nugget of wisdom that we should implement.

. . .

Strategy 5

5. Live below your means

Avoid lifestyle creep like the plague. Most people don't live below their means because doing the opposite is ingrained.

Consumerism is an unspoken and widespread addiction.

We are fed the following messages:

- We got to live the fabulous social media-worthy type lifestyle.

- We got to have the latest iPhone or iPad.

- We got to have a life *worth* imitating.

- We got to have the *things* we are taught to obtain to live a "fulfilling" life.

"So, concerning the things we pursue and for which we vigorously exert ourselves, we owe this consideration — either there is nothing useful in them, or most aren't useful. Some of them are superfluous, while others aren't worth that much.

But we don't discern this and see them as free when they cost us dearly." — The Daily Stoic p 75

. . .

Strategy 6

6. Enable your money to work for you through investing.

Investing allows you to utilize compound interest to your advantage, saving far more money than you could if you saved in a low-interest-rate savings account. The interest rates you receive from investing most often far outweigh any money you earn in a savings account.

Investing is both a critical and powerful tool. You don't have to have a degree in finance or economics to understand this. You don't have to be a financial genius to invest your money. All you need to do is find a solid, reputable financial firm or bank, or even start using your employer's 401k option (if you are working or have this benefit at your job) and start investing your money today.

. . .

Strategy 7

7. Consistently implement viable ideas to increase your income.

Something most people don't do is write down ideas when they come to mind. And since most people don't write down their goals, most do not write down 20 ideas — to help them reach their goals.

Earl Nightingale said it best, "Men simply don't think." Instead, they spend most of their time watching the tube and wake up one day and realize they're 65, and they've not tapped into their infinite potential by an inch.

Spend 10–15 minutes each day writing ideas to help you reach your goals faster. Some ideas will be mediocre, some will be great, and some will be legendary. Don't underestimate the power of an idea and writing things down.

Never cease increasing your income.

. . .

Strategy 8

8. Increase your income sources — especially passive income.

Depending upon one basket of income is like betting your life savings on **one** horse.

Maintaining multiple sources of income is one key to establishing a solid financial foundation (as far as income goes). None of us can ever predict the future 100%, so why do so many of us live as if we can?

What are your talents? What are you good at? What are you interested in? Be creative and find ways to capitalize on your talents and interests while also working your primary job(s). I suggest always having at least 3–10 different sources of income; if you find this to be too much to do, aim for a minimum of 2 different sources of income.

I guarantee that having multiple sources of income will:

1. Relieve financial pressure

2. Eradicate dependence on any one source of income or company

3. Give you more freedom

Passive income streams (e.g., royalties from books, music, and other intellectual property and real estate) are best because they generate money without you needing to invest time and effort consistently. Another popular option is to have a full-time gig and a part-time gig. **Again, never depend on one source of income.**

. . .

Strategy 9

9. <u>Educate</u> yourself on everything finance to inspire new ways of thinking.

If you're not learning, you're not growing.

Ignorance is not bliss. <u>Read as if your life depended on it</u>. The more you educate yourself, the better the life you'll experience.

Utilized knowledge is power.

. . .

Strategy 10

10. Surround yourself with wealthy individuals.

The majority doesn't have $500 in their bank account to cover an emergency expense, which means the majority is one step away from being broke or already broke. I'm not even taking into consideration the fact that most people are also in debt. Establish new relationships with individuals that can challenge your level of thinking and elevate your financial status.

. . .

Strategy 11

11. Engage in <u>entrepreneurship</u>, and work for yourself.

The best kind of job is where you're the boss, and you determine your earnings, schedule, benefits, income, and workload. Entrepreneurship gives you back the power to create your reality and set the tone for your financial future. At least one of your income sources should be from entrepreneurship.

. . .

Strategy 12

12. Embrace <u>minimalism</u>.

Implementing the practice of minimalism will ensure you don't buy things without a definite and meaningful reason.

I wrote an article called "<u>Desires Make You A Servant</u>" that belabors the idea:

If you want nothing, you have everything. You're in control, and no one has leverage over you. Not businesses, advertisements, societal "norms," people, or desires.

How often do we witness people buy the new car, only to watch them constantly work to pay for it?

They **have** to **keep** working, and if they don't, their car will be repossessed (not to mention their credit will get f*cked up).

Minimalism helps you avoid buying into the idea that you need to buy all the time, every day, and the things you don't need.

"[…] in a society of ever-bigger houses and ever more possessions: [..] there's a hidden cost to all of that accumulating." — The Daily Stoic p 75

Our health (financial, mental, physical,

emotional, and spiritual) and our peace are the

hidden costs.

Strategy 13

13. Study the top 1% of the wealthiest 1%; pick their brains.

Read articles and books, attend conferences, and learn from the top 1%. Not to attain the money they acquired but to learn what works and doesn't work for business, finance, investing, habits, productivity, and entrepreneurship.

. . .

Strategy 14

14. <u>Think</u> thoughts focusing on wealth, prosperity, and abundance.

Something you won't often hear from a wealthy person with a wealthy mentality is: "I'm broke." Wealthy people focus on prosperity, attracting more wealth, and think in terms of abundance.

. . .

Strategy 15

15. <u>Increase</u> your self-worth.

People with high self-worth do not settle for less in life. They believe they are worthy of financial independence. They negotiate higher pay, income, and salaries. They don't allow life to hand them whatever; they demand from life what they desire and create opportunities to succeed.

. . .

Strategy 16

16. Research and stay in tune.

The world and technology are moving fast.

Will your services be needed in the future? How will you earn a living in the future? Is your expertise becoming more valuable or less valuable?

Always think ahead and plan your next move.

Never become obsolete.

. . .

Strategy 17

17. Implement discipline.

Millionaires and financially successful people have made it to where they are because they are comfortable making sacrifices.

You will never reach financial independence if you don't know how to put off short-term pleasure for long-term goals.

I'm not suggesting you give up your favorite indulgence; I'm suggesting you consider the implications of all your habits. Be more intentional with your purposes. Are you collectively making purchases that detract from your financial goals?

Are you purchasing things impulsively that you don't really want?

Are you creating more debt or eradicating it?

Are you living below your means or living on the edge?

. . .

Strategy 18

18. Study Billionaires

You don't have to desire to be a billionaire to learn from them. You don't even have to like billionaires.

But they have more than a lesson or two to share with you about money.

Learn from these people. They are masters of attracting and creating money.

There is something you can learn from these unique individuals that will help you reach your financial goals.

. . .

Strategy 19

19. The More you learn, the more you earn.

In Strategy 9, we discuss education. And I bring up the topic again.

Never underestimate the value of education. The more you uplevel your financial IQ, the more you will inevitably earn. There is no way you cannot financially succeed and thrive as you acquire more financial knowledge.

When you know better, you do better.

Invest in your financial education with a determined and ferocious mindset.

I guarantee you will experience results you've never experienced previously. I know this because I saw it happen repeatedly in my life.

. . .

Strategy 20

20. <u>Never relinquish your financial independence.</u>

There will be times in our lives when we need other people to help us. Accept help when you need it and when you don't. But never become reliant on someone else to take care of you.

The financially independent can always take care of themselves -- even if they don't have to, and this ensures they **always** have options and are never subject to the financial control others can sometimes inflict.

. . .

Thank You For Reading

Thank you for reading this book.

Stay blessed, lucky, favored, aware, joyous, and committed to bettering yourself.

. . .

The End.

. . .

. . .

About Destiny S. Harris

Destiny S. Harris' goal is to positively inspire, cultivate, elevate, and educate the minds of individuals across the globe through her writing.

Creating (whether books, courses, articles, poetry, or music) has always been Destiny's thing, not to mention health & fitness and all things entrepreneurial. Destiny published her first book, "Beauty Secrets for Girls," at age 11 and her second book, "Don't Wait Until It's Too Late," at age 12.

Destiny obtained three degrees in Psychology, Political Science, & Cultural Studies. She also started her own music teaching business at the age of 14, which she led for over ten years. In addition, she has been teaching academic, career, and personal development topics to thousands of students and readers since 2004.

Outside of writing, Destiny loves and enjoys a few other things: reading, weightlifting, traveling, football, dogs, food, classic movies, mountain and ocean views, sleeping, plants, and nature.

Check out her work, leave a review, share your thoughts with your friends and family, and be a part of a movement: helping people learn and grow through means of self-education (books).

Complete the Steps To Get Free eBooks:

Step 1: Go to amazon.com/author/destinyharris

Step 2: Filter books by "Price: Low to High"

Step 3: Download available free books

. . .

Connect W/ Destiny S. Harris

Please reach out and stay in touch. Destiny S. Harris enjoys chatting with readers.

Start a conversation today @ destinyh.com

. . .

Free Gifts!

Access courses & free eBooks at the link below:

destinyh.com

. . .

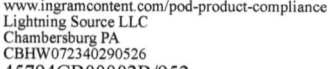